Sapere aude!

Ralph A. Hartmann

METATHEORIES
OF
LINGUISTICS

Saussure, Chomsky, and the
Reality Problem of Language

HARALEX **Publishing House**
Edinburgh
2018

HARALEX Publishing House
3 Wardlaw Place
Edinburgh EH11 1UA

Published 2018 by *HARALEX* Publishing House

This paperback edition (2018)
ISBN: 9781723786013

Contents

1. Introduction

1.1. The "nature" of language –
the reality problem (of language)

It might seem questionable to some linguists to deal with metalinguistics, i.e. with a metatheory or rather philosophy of linguistics. A sensible and serious researcher, however, should be keen to get clarification about what subject matter he investigates, about which premises he bases his research on or, basically, about what the nature of the object he studies actually is. Katz (1985:11) calls the latter aspect in respect of linguistics the "ontological" problem of language which he sees as the main topic of the philosophy of linguistics, and which consequently is the topic of the contributions to his anthology (Katz 1985). A metatheory of linguistics therefore starts with the "ontological" problem or, to use an alternative term, the reality problem which, according to Katz, asks the question whether sentences or rather languages are physical, psychological or abstract objects. This division into three of the respective positions of nominalism, conceptualism or realism, however, has to be seen in relative terms, as the following discussion will clearly show.

1.2. Saussure's reality problem

It is also at the start of Ferdinand de Saussure's theoretical foundations of linguistics that we find the reality problem in the shape of the sentence "C'est le point de vue qui crée l'objet" which tells us that it is the perspective, the viewpoint of the linguist that creates the object of linguistic studies. Not least through this sentence, which plays a key role within Saussure's lectures written down and edited by his students posthumously, the scholar from Geneva managed to influence the following history of linguistics with a long lasting effect – be it in the form of severe criticism appearing in numerous writings provoked by his conception of language, or as approval of his opinions in at least as many instances.

1.3. Chomsky's critique of Saussure

The long list of those casting criticism upon Saussure's hypotheses also contains the name Noam Chomsky. Chomsky, whose contributions to the academic study of language in the 20th century are very often regarded as a shift of paradigms, undisputably acknowledges Saussure's merits as far as the discipline of linguistics is concerned, but at the same time he also rejects Saussure's conception of language mainly by means of the accusation that Saussure had pursued mere inventory or corpus linguistics.

1.4. Programme

In the course of the discussion here, Saussure's and Chomsky's systems are being compared contrastively in order to prove eventually that these two most important approaches to linguistics are very well compatible and, once unified, may ultimately form a much more plausible theoretical foundation of linguistics as each one on its own. This claim naturally presupposes the assumption that Saussure's thoughts on language still have to be considered as modern, a viewpoint which Chomsky would vehemently deny. Furthermore, Katz's division of the philosophy of linguistics into three as briefly mentioned above, will also be considered because he categorizes Chomsky and Saussure in a way which - at least in Saussure's case – is highly doubtful.

2. Saussure and Chomsky: Competition or compatibility?

2.1. Saussure in keywords

If Saussure's conception of language has to be summarized in keywords, we only have to have a look at his striking and original terminology. What we encounter here are concepts like his division of language into LANGUE (= language), PAROLE (≈ speaking), and LANGAGE (≈ human speech). We can also find the characterization of language as a heritage, as a convention, as a historical, social, and even psychological fact, as a system of signs which has to be described within the framework of a theory of signs ("semiology") and in consideration of a conceptual triangle consisting of the notions "sign" (*signe*), "signifier" (*signifiant*), and "signified" (*signifié*) as well as of the aspect of a sign's arbitrariness (*arbitraire du signe*). Last but not least, Saussure's vision of an exemplary and scientifically based study of language split into the two parts of synchrony and diachrony might strike the eye, too.

2.2. Language's division into three

In respect of the contrastive analysis of Saussure's and Chomsky's systems, the main focus with regards to the discussion of Saussure's theory shall be put on his sociologism as well as on the concepts of LANGAGE, PAROLE, and LANGUE as it is especially at that point where we can see parallels with Chomsky who, similarly, distinguishes between competence and performance.

But first to Saussure, who assumes that the phenomenon of language shows three different aspects; first, there is LANGAGE which, according to Saussure, cannot be classified, which also represents the physical, psychological, and physiological component of language, and which, in its nature, has a social as well as an individual side. Not least due to its classifiability,

LANGUE is the more important part of language for Saussure, i.e. "a social product of the faculty of" LANGAGE (cf Saussure 1959/ 1966:9). LANGUE is that part of language which mainly makes language a social fact. It is at this point where we can see

> "a collection of necessary conventions that have been adopted by a social body to permit individuals to exercise that faculty. " (Saussure 1959/1966:9)

Finally, there is also the aspect of PAROLE, which refers to the actual instances of speaking as such, i.e. single speech acts, acts of listening, or the results of the speech acts (=utterances) respectively. Generalizing roughly, we can detect analogies to Saussure's division of language within Chomsky's theoretical premises, meaning that Saussure's LANGUE would correspond to Chomsky's COMPETENCE who, with this term, refers to an idealized speaker-listener's knowledge of language. Furthermore, Saussure's PAROLE would be comparable to Chomsky's PERFORMANCE, which characterizes the actual use of language in concrete situations (cf Chomsky 1965:81). Finally, one could possibly identify Chomsky's concept of a UNIVERSAL GRAMMAR (UG) with Saussure's LANGAGE as UG is defined as the theory of the initial state of the language faculty. UG thus is an individual's physical, psychological, and physiological predisposition for language. Such a predisposition exists before all linguistic experience / input.

2.3. Chomsky's basic concepts: E- and I-language, MI and MC

Chomsky is not very much interested in what he labels "performance". He just takes it for granted and puts the main emphasis of his reflections on competence and UG, which is why D'Agostino (1986:14) calls him a methodological individualist. Chomsky mentions the social component of language only marginally (cf Chomsky 1986: 18), which, on the other hand, is Saussure's focus of attention. Chomsky anyway thinks that one has to decide between either a linguistic sociologism following Saussure or his own methodological individualism, which, in turn, only allows for a neurobiological and a psychological variant. For Chomsky, a synthesis of both positions as proposed here, is simply not possible.

Chomsky distinguishes between an "externalized language" (E-language) and an "internalized language" (I-language), subsuming the aspect of language as a social fact under E-language, i.e. an area in which the construct of language is considered to be independent of the "mind/brain". Chomsky's theoretical starting point, however, is I-language, i.e. an element of a person's mind who knows (the) language, and therefore also a neuronal as well as a psychological fact. In contrast to that, E-languages are – at least according to Chomsky – not factual as such, but only derived and therefore further away from the data, mechanisms as well as grammars (= theories of I-languages) than I-languages. Chomsky speaks of a shift of focus and interest from E-language to I-language, which he would like to see even more enforced. This shift of interest, in Chomsky's opinion, corresponds to a "movement" from behaviour and its products to the cognitive system which feeds into behaviour. It is here that we notice Chomsky's uncompromising attitude very clearly, which can be seen in stark contrast to Saussure's relative openness towards an additional individualistic interpretation of his principally sociological system. D'Agostino (1986) has the same view on this matter when he distinguishes between methodological individualism (MI) and methodological collectivism / sociologism (MC): while the methods of MI locate the phenomenon of language mainly in the mind or rather the neurobiology of an individual, MC quite adversely locates language in society which is taken to be a fact. Yet, MC also leaves space for considering the mental, psychological, neuronal, or physical aspect of language. Language interpreted as social fact would by no means exclude such an aspect. To recap the contrast: while MI excludes any kind of sociologism categorically, MC acknowledges the importance of individualism to a quite considerable extent. This kind of "asymmetry", according to D'Agostino (1986:15f), makes it more difficult for the critic to refute MC compared to MI. However, it should not be the point to exclude or refute either of the positions, but rather to recognize the fact that there are sociological as well as neuronal / mental origins or foundations of the phenomenon of language.

2.4. Sociologism and transmissibility

The "social aspect" of language which Saussure suggests, is undisputable. Furthermore, we have to concede that language is being passed on from generation(s) to generation(s), i.e. interwoven with the social side of language is its historical aspect. The keyword here is that of transmissibility, even if it cannot be one hundred percent precise, and very often underlies "disturbances" as e.g. phonetic tendencies. Language acquisition and learning, at least as far as the lexicon is concerned, is therefore very much dependent on the cultural environment; it is the inventory of words valid in a specific speech community that is being learnt. The vocabulary shows relative stability over a shorter period of time. Over a longer period of time, however, it changes, and we are very well able to document this change by means of explicit phonetic tendencies or rules.

We are even able to find the aspect of transmissibility in Chomsky's system, namely when we consider his so-called parameters. Chomsky sees UG as consisting of different sub-systems of principles as e.g. X-bar-theory, theta-theory, binding theory, and a few more. Such principles constitute single "language modules" of UG[1]. It is exactly these principles, in turn, which are connected to parameters which have to be strengthened or fixed through experience, or more precisely by means of relatively simple data. Once the values of the pa-

---

[1] Corresponding modular structures, as Chomsky (1986:146) emphasizes, can frequently be found when studying cognitive systems. Not least for that reason it seems plausible that Chomsky considers linguistics to be a sub-discipline of (cognitive) psychology (see D'Agostino 1986:11).

rameters are set, the whole system (i.e. the language in question) is working. The values of the parameters therefore have to be "delivered" by society or, more precisely, by the speech community. The child acquiring language then processes and, at the same time, consolidates these values. At this point, we could somehow speak of a certain sociological aspect in Chomsky's system, but he himself would strongly deny that as he, in contrast to Saussure, puts the emphasis on the principles mentioned earlier and consequently on the mental or rather neuronal predisposition for language. For Saussure, the data provided by the speech community have more weight, and this extends to the synchronic aspect as well as to the diachronic (i.e. historical) side (referring to the transmissibility of the lexicon).

2.5. Chomsky-conclusion, S_0 and S_S, principles and parameters

According to the so-called Chomsky-conclusion, the common typological features of languages may be explained through the common capacity for language (acquisition) of all humans. Chomsky considers the language faculty as a separate and own system of the "mind/ brain" with an "initial state" (S_0), which is species-specific for humans. It should also be noted in this context that UG is taken to be the theory of S_0. Provided that there is an appropriate level of experience given, this language faculty develops from state S_0 into a relatively stable "steady state" (S_S), which then only underlies very few peripheral modifications as e.g. acquisition of new vocabulary items. The state attained includes an I-language. Specific grammars are thus

theories of different I-languages. I-languages which can be attained presupposing a
fixed state S_0 and varying experience, are
the set of hypothetically attainable human
languages. I-language therefore consists of
two components: on the one side there is
the contribution of S_0, on the other side we
have the specific characteristics of the respective language which ultimately is being
acquired (see Chomsky 1986:25/26). In sim-
plified terms (the concepts of principles
and parameters included in our considera-
tions), this means the following: (1) we are
equipped with an innate knowledge of the
principles of the different sub-systems of S_0
as well as with the parameters linked to the
principles, (2) we learn the values of the
parameters and thus constitute a so-called
"core language" which is extended by elements of the periphery, i.e. by anything
else added to the system and represented

in the "mind/brain" of the speaker-listener. The language we then know is a system of principles with fixed parameters together with a periphery of marked exceptions. All this cannot be seen as a system of rules in the conventional sense (see Chomsky 1986: 150)

2.6. Weaknesses in Chomsky's conception of language

Scrutinizing this, we may easily spot a few hick-ups especially in those areas which deal with learning. Chomsky e.g. speaks of a so-called periphery with exceptions such as irregular morphology and slangs, which basically just reflect social facts. Naturally, Chomsky wishes to exclude this, and as things like that make all his techniques (developed on the basis of such exclusive assumptions) highly questionable, he devalues the relevance of such social facts and classifies them as peripheral or insignificant. He makes a decisive idealization assuming an ideal speaker-listener within a homogeneous speech community who knows his language perfectly and cannot be influenced by grammatically irrelevant conditions such as a limited memory, distractions, changes of attention and interest as well as (coincidental or characteristic) mistakes while applying his knowledge of language within actual use (performance).

Apart from idealizations like that, the data Chomsky bases his linguistic techniques on, seem to be quite questionable: he looks at grammaticality judgements of adult speakers (of English) regarding not too many (English) sentences, in order to "fiddle around" with his principles and parameters so that these are compatible with the respective judgements. In the tradition of Generative Grammar, and here especially within Transformational Grammar, numerous research papers strike the eye which deal with the "improvement" of single principles in great detail only with being revised after a short period to be levelled with other data, i.e. other grammaticality judgements. This kind of "method" very much reminds of endeavours in early modern astronomy controlled by clerics, when it came to sustain the validity of the geocentric conception of the world technically by construeing ever more complicated epicycles of planet movements. However, as Chomsky insists quite severely, the linguistic technique of Generative Grammar allegedly fulfills both requirements – adequacy in respect of description as well as of explanation - he himself demands of a scientific theory (cf Chomsky 1986:43). If we believe Chomsky, a linguistic theory like Saussure's, in turn, lacks adequacy of explanation.

2.7. Adequacy of description and explanation in Saussure's system

Such a generalization, which accuses a socio-historical view like Saussure's of being inadequate in respect of explanation, must not be made without any further reflection. Saussure's alternative to Chomsky's method would be an undoubtedly explanative model based on historical phonology whereby words to be compared with each other would be listed, similarities as e.g. phonetic correspondences would be registered, and protoforms as well as phonological rules would be reconstructed. As can be seen, this method refers back to the lexicon. And as has previously been shown, transmissibility of the lexicon is a fact which has to be explained. Saussure's methodology then takes us to a model which corresponds to historical phonology. The explanative character of such a model is e.g. based on the fact that phonological rules – seen from a mathematical perspective - are calculable total functions.

2.7.1. The linguistic sign

It is not merely Saussure's emphasis of language being a social as well as a historical fact which takes us to such a model of explanation. We rather have to consider Saussure's conception (of language) as a whole. For that purpose, it is basically necessary to clarify what Saussure takes to be a sign, as his theory's central notion is the one of the sign and has not been discussed here so far. Saussure calls "the combination of a concept and a sound-image a *sign*" (Saussure 1959/1966:67) clarifying later that "concept" should rather be "signified" (*signifié*), and that "sound-image" would have to be replaced by "signifier" (*signifiant*). But as is almost self-evident, the signified does usually have different signifiers in different languages, and we therefore may conclude:

"The bond between the signifier and the signified is arbitrary", or

"*the linguistic sign is arbitrary.*" (both quotes from Saussure 1959/1966:67)

2.8. Saussure's system as an index card model of language

After Saussure's idea of the sign has been clarified, we may now summarize his entire conception of language as some kind of index card model as proposed by Egli & Egli-Gerber (1992:51). According to this model, language is a multi-dimensional continuum which can be seen in analogy to index cards: the first dimension (top and bottom on the card) would correspond to structural categorization which consists of a relation of dominance running from top to bottom on the one side, and of a relation of abstraction running from bottom to top, whereby at the bottom – which would also be the most dominated as well as the most concrete stage – we would have the level of words (e.g. the sentence or the utterance "Women cook"). One stage further up we would have the level of parts of speech (in the case of "Women cook" this would be N (= noun) + V (= verb)). One stage further up in the degree of abstraction, this would be followed by the so-called immediate constituents (NP (= noun phrase) + VP (= verb phrase)). The highest level of abstraction then would be the one of sentences (S). The second dimension (right and left side of the index card) would correspond to Saussure's principle of "linéarité du signe", i.e. the temporal level. In the third dimension we would encounter the relationship between *signifiant* and *signifié*, which would correspond to the front and reverse side of the index card. The fourth dimension would comprise Saussure's concepts of LANGUE and PAROLE, whereby we would have to imagine that, in our model, LANGUE would correspond to the whole of (a finite number of) basic index cards, whereas PA-

ROLE would have to be understood as individual cards which, probably to a large part, are put together anew. The fifth dimension, in turn, would consist of associative links which could be compared to cross references between cards existing at the same time. The sixth and last dimension would correspond to diachrony which, in our model, would have to be understood as the relation of one card to another different card of an earlier stage.

2.9. Categorization

If we interpret Saussure's system in a way as the index card model suggests, the emphasis on the first dimension, i.e. categorization, is striking. It is also at this precise point where traditional grammar, Saussure as well as modern phrase structure grammar may be reconciled: anyone who has ever learned or who is ever going to learn a foreign language would approve of the usefulness of a traditional grammar of the respective language to be learned when it comes to making learning progress easier. This is because such a grammar (as e.g. the *Hammer Grammar* of English or the *Dudengrammatik* of German) does not just list the concrete matters to be learned in the form of rules or principles; it rather categorizes as e.g. within the inflectional paradigms of morphology. Consequently, Egli

& Egli-Gerber (1992:133) propagate a phrase structure grammar which shifts the focus away from rules and principles (in a Chomskyan sense) towards categorization. This is made plausible by the observation that learners of foreign languages rather learn the categorization of linguistic elements than rules. Furthermore, we may distance ourselves a little bit from the idea of universal grammar by interpreting categorization as being determined largely by the specific language in question, or even by society (speech community), by history as well as by culture. However, Universal Grammar as well as Chomskyan nativism is by no means forgotten as we simply have to assume a biologically as well as neurologically predetermined scope of possibility for languages which corresponds to the idea of Universal Grammar. But with regards to the evolution of mankind and thus the evolution of language or the language faculty for that matter, such a scope of possibility has to be seen as a constantly developing rather than a fixed factor defining the human species. Language itself in its actual usage as well as the predisposition for language underlies the influence of time. This is why a technical description of or an investigation into the human predisposition for language may very well be wished for, but it also has to be said that such an endeavour is extremely difficult. In any case, we may assume that there **is** a human predisposition for language. It also may, however, always remain a mystery to us how this predisposition has developed in the course of the millennia.

3. The reality problem according to Katz

3.1. Three different positions

But let us, at this point, come back to the problem of reality which asks the question about the ontological status of language. Katz's anthology (Katz 1985) is an important contribution to the discussion of this problem. There we can find a division into three as far as contrasting positions towards the problem of reality are concerned. Accordingly, the nominalists L. Bloomfield, Z. Harris, and W. V. Quine understand sentences or languages as physical objects, the conceptualists E. Sapir, N. Chomsky, S. Stich, and J. Fodor, in turn, interpret languages as psychological objects, whereas the realists L. Hjelmslev, J. Katz himself, S. Soames, D.T. Langendoen, and P.M. Postal are of the opinion that languages are abstract objects. This is, of course, a very rough summary of the single positions, which are intended to be outlined by using Bloomfield's and Katz's argumentation as well as Hjelmslev's "realistic" interpretation of Saussure as some kind of examples. Chomsky's conceptualism, however, need not be discussed here again as this was done above in greater detail.

3.1.1. Bloomfield's nominalism

Leonard Bloomfield, one of the most prominent figures representing American Structuralism within linguistics, made a very basic premise at the starting point of his work, namely the assumption that a speaker produced "noise". The linguist, according to Bloomfield, therefore did not have any choice but to show in detail that a speaker did not have any "ideas" and that the study of the "noise" produced by language was sufficient as it was the speaker's words which influenced the nerve systems of his fellow speakers through some kind of trigger effect (see Katz 1985:23). Furthermore, it had to be considered that it was merely the verbal act to be constant from person to person. Consequently, the term "idea" could only be seen as a traditional and obscure synonym for "speech-form". What commonly was understood as "mental event" therefore was nothing else than private and irrelevant events of physiology on the one side, and social events, i.e. speech acts (see Katz 1985:25), on the other side.

3.1.2. Katz's Platonistic realism

Katz himself propagates a Platonistic view. He thinks that grammars have to be understood as theories on sentence structure. These sentences exist as abstract objects in a similar way as Platonists in the philosophy of mathematics comprehend numbers. Accordingly, they are neither considered to be located in physical space as sound waves or even stains of ink, nor are they interpreted as mental events or states occurring at any one time in any one subject. Katz understands sentences as entities whose structure we may discover by means of intuition and reason rather than through perception and induction (see Katz 1985:173). In Katz's opinion, we would encounter the difficulty of separating linguistics from the cognitive sciences if we considered linguistics to be a part of psychology (as Chomsky does). In contrast to this, Katz is convinced that we would not come across difficulties like that if we held a Platonistic position. Opposing conceptualism, Katz claims that conditions of psychological reality within linguistics do not refer to the grammatical structure of sentences, but to specifics of subjective experience or of human biology (see Katz 1985:195).

3.1.3. Hjelmslev's realism

Hjelmslev's basis for interpreting Saussure's conception of language is Saussure's comparison of a game of chess with language (Saussure 1959/1966:88/89). According to this metaphor used by Saussure, a chessman is exclusively determined by its relation to the other chessmen as well as by its relative position on the chessboard, whereas the form or appearance of the chessman and also the material it is made of, are not substantial to the game itself. Comparable to Katz, Hjelmslev's method is a structural(istic) approach to language. He names this kind of linguistics *glossematics*. In his interpretation of the concept of structure, Hjelmslev explicitly refers back to Rudolf Carnap who, in line with a "realistic" view of things, considers structure as a purely formal and relational fact. Hjelmslev's mentioning of Saussure's comparison of language with a game of chess and its formal / relational character now suggests that he interprets him in exactly the same way. With an interpretation like that, however, Hjelmslev fails to see that Saussure explicitly understood language as a mental and mainly as a social fact – in addition to its formal / relational character. To classify

Saussure as a realist in Katz's sense therefore does not match the facts.

3.2. Critique of Katz's categorization; alternative suggestion

In general, we have to accuse Katz of not having interpreted the respective linguists accurately. Furthermore, it seems highly questionable whether the philosophy of mathematics is also applicable to linguistics, as the kind of realism which is applicable to mathematical systems cannot be applied to language, because the phenomenon of the validity of the sign-relation "given through the character of language as a sociological fact" (see Egli & Egli-Gerber 1992:53 [translation R.H.]) has to be integrated as well. We thus also have to consider some kind of realism which refers to empirical abstract objects and not exclusively to "mathematical" abstract objects – i.e. the mathematical reconstruction of empirical abstract objects. The position propagated by Katz himself may be criticised in respect of him ignoring the socio-historical aspect of language. Quite apart from that, the psychological aspect is only represented in the data, but not in theory. And last but not least, Katz also neglects the correlation between structure and sound.

It basically seems to be too simplistic to assume a division into three positions as far as the problem of reality is concerned. We could rather see the ontological problem of language in three contrasting dichotomies or even dimensions which are still reconcilable: (1) Cultural-historical dimension in contrast to biological-psychological dimension, (2) realism in contrast to nativism / conceptualism, (3) sociologism in contrast to individualism.

3.3. Influence of data
on theory formation

When the question of language's ontological status arises, it is therefore possible to give different answers. Yet, these "solutions" of the problem of reality are strongly influenced by the data we base our research on. Consequently, there are four kinds of data defining the respective position. A comparative study of the lexicon thus takes us to etymology and historical linguistics, i.e. to the interpretation of language as an institution, and ultimately to sociologism. The author mainly associated with this position of sociologism would be Ferdinand de Saussure. However, if we undertake a comparative study of syntax, it will take us to typology and thus to the theory of Universal Grammar. This would correspond to Chomskyan conceptualism and/ or nativism. And while a comparative investigation into semantics represents the linguistic method of a (Platonistic) realism following Katz and Montague, a linguist like Leonard Bloomfield, who propagates nominalism or rather some kind of nominalistic realism, deals with a comparative study of sounds.

Yet, we have to make sure that data must not be selected in a one-sided manner, because language belongs to numerous areas of reality which have to be considered. If we just list sound events, intuitive judgements (of speakers) on well-formedness of sentences, neurophysiological data, and acts of articulation or rather speech acts, we have only covered but a very few of the most important areas of reality language belongs to.

It is also plausible to state that linguistic structures match exactly the invariant features of the different areas of reality, as a certain isomorphy of articulation as well as of sound event with neurophysiological or rather mental structures can be found.

3.4. A synthesis of fundamental theories

As shown by the above discussion, seemingly contrasting positions concerning the problem of reality may not exclude each other. Consequently, if we seriously intend to pursue an academic study of language that describes and explains at the same time, we require the social as well as the individual aspect of language. This, however, makes it impossible to ascribe a correspondence of Chomskyan COMPETENCE to Saussurean LANGUE, because COMPETENCE mainly deals with the individual aspect of language, whereas LANGUE emphasizes the social aspect of language. A roughly generalized correspondence of COMPETENCE to LANGUE as assumed at the start of the discussion here therefore has to be abandoned in the framework of linguistics considered to be an adequate academic study of language. Linguistics as a sensible research discipline must therefore also include attempts to describe adult linguistic competence as well as the language faculty's initial state of a child. And finally, it is also obligatory to consider the formal as well as the content side of language.

4. Summary

In view of the multitude of aspects outlined and evaluated in the course of our discussion, it seems quite appropriate to summarize the most important issues of an adequate metatheory of linguistics again:

It was already at the very beginning that we were confronted with the problem of reality concerning language in the form of the claim "C'est le point de vue qui crée l'objet". This made us analyse Ferdinand de Saussure's and Noam Chomsky's conceptions of language.

The most important aspects striking the eye within Saussure's theory were his trichotomy of LANGAGE, LANGUE, and PAROLE, his opinion that language is a social fact, his consideration of transmissibility within the historical side of language as well as his conceding the possibility to interpret language as a psychological fact. Saussure's division of linguistics (as a sensible research discipline to be taken seriously in an academic context) into diachrony and synchrony was also outlined, and, after that, his whole conception of language was interpreted using an index card model.

The portrayal of Noam Chomsky's conception of language included his idealization of the perfect speaker-listener, his conclusion that there is an innate faculty of language (acquisition) by assuming universal / widespread (grammatical) features of languages, his peculiar data in the form of grammar judgements of (non-perfect) speaker-listeners, and his insisting that Generative Grammar is adequate as far as description and explanation are concerned. Furthermore, in order to understand Chomsky's fundamental view of language, it was essential to clarify distinctions like competence vs. performance, E-language vs. I-language, "initial state" vs. "steady state" as well as technical concepts like principles and parameters.

In the course of the comparison of Saussure with Chomsky it became clear already that a one-sided, individualistic conception of language is not desirable. A discussion of the problem of reality following the anthology of Katz (1985) consequently strengthened the claim that a multi-dimensional conception of language comprising all areas of reality language belongs to, points to a more adequate answer to the question about the ontological status of language, and also seems to be more useful for the general understanding of linguistics or rather for the way linguists perceive their subject.

5. References

Chomsky, Noam (1965): Methodological Preliminaries. In: Katz, J.J. (1985). 80-125.

Chomsky, Noam (1966): Cartesian Linguistics. A Chapter in the History of Rationalist Thought. New York / London.

Chomsky, Noam (1982): On the Generative Enterprise. Dordrecht (NL).

Chomsky, Noam (1986): Knowledge of Language. New York / Westport (Connecticut) / London.

D'Agostino, Fred (1986): Chomsky's System of Ideas. Oxford.

Egli, Urs / Egli-Gerber, Renata (1992): Sprachsysteme - logische und historische Grundlagen der erweiterten Phrasenstrukturgrammatik. Arbeitspapier Nr. 28 der Fachgruppe Sprachwissenschaft der Universität Konstanz. 2. Auflage. Konstanz.

Katz, Jerrold J., Hrsg. (1985): The Philosophy of Linguistics. Oxford.

Saussure, Ferdinand de (1959 / 1966): Course in General Linguistics (translated, with an introduction and notes by Wade Baskin). New York/Toronto/London.

The author

Dr. Ralph A. Hartmann was born in Leutkirch/Allgäu (Germany) in 1966. He studied at the universities of Konstanz (Germany) and Cork (Republic of Ireland). He is a graduated philosopher and holds a doctorate in linguistics. He taught linguistics and German as a foreign language at the universities of Konstanz, St Andrews (Scotland), Witwatersrand (Johannesburg, South Africa) and Manchester (England). Since 2002 he has been residing in Scotland's capital Edinburgh running a Language Consultancy and Philosophical Practice.

Other texts on philosophy and/or linguistics by Ralph A. Hartmann available as KINDLE e-books:

*PHILOSOPHIES OF
LANGUAGE AND LINGUISTICS:
Plato, Aristotle, Saussure, Wittgenstein, Bloomfield,
Russell, Quine, Searle, Chomsky, and Pinker on
Language and its Systematic Study*
(e-book as well as paperback)

*LINGUETHICA MATERIALISTICA
From Fact (Is) to Virtue (Ought)*
(e-book as well as paperback)

*ESCAPE FROM MYTHOLOGY:
The Pre-Socratic Philosophers
and their Understanding of Nature*
(e-book as well as paperback)

*MAN - A LANGUAGE MACHINE?:
Chomsky and Piaget on Linguistic Nativism*
(e-book as well as paperback)

*THE EVOLUTION OF EPISTEMOLOGY
TO EVOLUTIONARY EPISTEMOLOGY:
Two modern re-interpretations of Immanuel Kant's
fundamental principles of Transcendental Philosophy*
(e-book as well as paperback)

Printed in Great Britain
by Amazon